Easy-to-Use Sermon Outline Series

D0897226

Sermons Outlines
For
Funeral Services

compiled by

Charles R. Wood

KREGEL PUBLICATIONS
Grand Rapids, Michigan 49501

Sermon Outlines for Funeral Services, compiled by
Charles R. Wood. Copyright © 1970 by Kregel Publications, a division of Kregel, Inc. All rights reserved. No
part of this book may be reproduced in any form or by
any mechanical means, including duplicating machine and
tape recorder, without permission in writing from the
publisher.

ISBN 0-8254-4007-6

5 6 7 8 9 Printing/Year 90 89 88 87

Printed in the United States of America.

Contents

Textual Index

Preface

The appropriate word at the moment of bereavement is both an absolute necessity and a difficult choice. The funeral usually comes upon the preacher without warning and often catches him at an inopportune time when the press of duties makes adequate preparation almost impossible. The sermon outlines in this book are designed to meet both needs — the need for an appropriate word and the need for a message which can be used with a minimum of preparation.

The messages herein are designed to have a dual impact, both to comfort the saints and to evangelize. Although many of them fit into one of these categories alone, a number of them are adapted to either purpose and can easily be presented with a twofold application.

The compiler has taken into account the ever-trying task of preaching a worthy sermon at the service for the man of whose destiny he is not sure. Several sermons have been included which are sufficiently general to allow use in such "unsure" situations.

Many of the included messages are the compiler's own and have had fairly frequent use. A portion of them, however, have been borrowed from a number of sources. Where it has been possible to determine the identity of the original author, he has been credited. Where this has not been possible, the term "adapted" has been used to indicate borrowing from an unknown source.

Actually "adapted" is very accurate because all the sermons from other sources have been brought up to date and streamlined for ease of usage.

It is the compiler's prayer that this volume may significantly add to the "preacher's sermon barrel" and that the sermons in it may be used to bring comfort to the sorrowing and to make some "wise unto salvation".

The Bright Side Of Death

NUMBERS 23:10

Introduction:

Most persons look upon death as a dark and gloomy thing without one redeeming quality. But the death of the righteous, like the towering clouds that shut out the sun at noonday, has a bright side and a silver lining also.

I. **Dying Is Not So Painful As Is Commonly Supposed.**
    A. True to our natural instincts, we shrink back from death.
    B. The experience and research of many would indicate to us that death is not normally a painful or traumatic experience.

II. **Many Deaths Are Very Bright.**
    A. The death of the righteous is extremely bright when compared with the death of the wicked.
    B. In fact, we can say that far greater misfortune than death can befall or overtake the Christian.

III. **Death Is Not A Forfeiture Of Conscious Being.**
    A. Our intelligent and spiritual parts are imperishable.
    B. Death does not destroy the inhabitant; it only takes down the house in which he lives.

IV. **Death Leads To A Resurrection Body.**
    A. Man was created for immortality, and he shall arise from the grave and live forever.
    B. Death shall be destroyed for the Christian because, "this mortal must put on immortality."

V. **Death Is The Way To The Betterment Of The Christian's Estate.**
    A. It is the soul's emancipation from all bondage and limitations that mar its larger pleasures and deter its expansion and unfolding.
    B. It secures the believer an immediate increase of all that is good in itself. It is going from large opportunities to larger ones.
    C. It is recovery of and everlasting reunion with departed loved ones.

Conclusion:

Beneath the dark cloud of death we often cringe. Let us be aware of the fact that the dark cloud of death but opens the door to the bright glories of heaven.

—R. Rock

Faith And Hope In Job

JOB 19:25-27

Introduction:

Although Job was weighed down by a heavy load of afflictions and misrepresented by his mistaken friends, he looked forward to the coming of his Redeemer. He had a comfortable assurance that his Redeemer would avenge his wrongs, raise him from the dead and bless him with the beatific vision.

I. **Job Had A Living Redeemer.**
   A. The work of a Redeemer is great and highly important.
      1. He pays the price for the lost possession of his brother.
      2. He saves and delivers his brother.
      3. He vindicates and avenges his brother.
   B. Christ is the great Redeemer of Men.
      1. He bought us with His blood.
      2. He saves and delivers His people from the guilt, power and polution of sin.
      3. He will vindicate and avenge His church.
   C. The Son of God, our great Redeemer, was living in the days of Job.
      1. He had a saving interest in Job and what he was enduring.
      2. Job recognized the fact of his preincarnate existence.
   D. Job knew his divine Redeemer.
      1. It could have been tradition that gave Job this information.
      2. It is much more likely that God gave him understanding as a result of direct divine revelation.

II. **Job Thought His Affliction Would Terminate In Death.**
   A. When he spoke the words of his text, his skin was destroyed.
      1. The Lord had allowed him to be greatly afflicted.
      2. He was actually able to peel some of the skin off his body.

B. After the destruction of his skin, he expected his whole body to be destroyed.
C. Death and the grave, with their solemn attendants, closed every earthly prospect of that deeply afflicted and eminently holy man.
 1. Job seemed to be facing certain death and viewed things that way.
 2. We too face certain death and ought to view things that way.

III. Job Had A Joyful Hope Of A Resurrection From The Dead.
A. He positively affirmed that he would see God after the destruction of his flesh.
 1. This would simply not be possible if the dead rise not.
 2. The fact is that God will raise the dead although we do not know the specific method He will use to do so.
 3. This has been proved by the resurrection of Jesus and provides us with great hope.
B. He further affirmed that the vision would be personal and absolutely real (". . . mine eyes shall behold, and not another.")
 1. He felt he would see Him and Him enjoy for himself.
 2. His confidence in the Redeemed was along these lines:
  a. He will deliver me from death and the grave.
  b. He will vindicate my character.
  c. He will avenge my foes.

Conclusion:
Jesus has been the hope of pious men in all ages because He is the great Redeemer promised by the Bible who is able to do all that could be asked or expected by a Redeemer.

—Adapted

When The Lights Go Out

PSALM 10:1

Introduction:
It is a common experience in the face of death to feel as if the very light of life has gone out for us. This happened to David at some point in his experience, and he said some things which we might do well to remember.

I. **This Is A Common Experience.**
   A. Psalmist has just been through an upset.
      1. It had affected his feelings toward the Lord.
         a. God seemed distant.
         b. God seemed unaware of his troubles.
      2. This was a fairly common experience for David. (Cf. Psalm 13:1; 22:1; 35:22 & 23, etc.)
   B. We share the same experience.
      1. This feeling hits all age groups and types.
      2. It most often manifests itself in depressive feelings.

II. **This Experience Causes Us To Lose Perspective.**
   A. Illustrated by Elijah. (I Kings 19:1-4)
      1. He had known triumph but now was emotionally and physically drained.
      2. He lost perspective and was ready to quit.
   B. This is so applicable to us.
      1. The lights go out for reasons such as sorrow.
      2. This tends to cause us to lose perspective and get overly morbid and pessimistic.

III. **This Experience Is More Apparent Than Real.**
   A. Illustrated by Elisha. (II Kings 6:13-17)
      1. The city is surrounded by a great company, and the young man was terrified.
      2. Elisha could see the ever-present, unseen hosts of the Lord.
   B. This is so applicable to us.
      1. We tend to focus in on trouble and to see only it.
      2. We need to remember that the unseen presence of the Lord is ever with us.

IV. **This Experience Is Often By A Great Revelation Of His Person.**
    A.   Illustrated by disciples. (Luke 24:13-31)
        1.   Time of darkest night with Messiah and hopes both dead.
        2.   He reveals Himself to them in their misery.
    B.   This is also applicable to us.
        1.   God has promised to deliver — when things get bleak, break must come.
        2.   This should encourage us in sorrow.

V. **This Experience Reminds Us Of What Christ Suffered.**
    A.   Illustrated in His life. (Mark 15:33-35)
        1.   He knew the sense of separation we know at death.
        2.   He cried out to the Father in the midst of it.
    B.   This is also applicable to us.
        1.   We can be sure He knows what it is like and can sense something of the agony He suffered.
        2.   This should make us thankful for our experience as it causes us to appreciate Him more.

Conclusion:
When the lights go out, remember the teaching of this Biblical consideration. It may help us through the darkest hour.

The Lessons Of Life And Death

PSALM 90:12

Introduction:
Wisdom is a most valuable possession, more to be desired, sought after and prized than any earthly thing. The Scriptures estimate the worth of it and recommend finding it above all other things and at any price.

I. **The Nature Of Wisdom Considered**
   A. Wisdom is distinguished from mere knowledge in that wisdom presupposes knowledge:
      1. It implies the right use of knowledge.
      2. It is most directly related to total content of knowledge.
   B. Wisdom is derived from God when it is true wisdom. That which only comes from man is not really true wisdom at all.
   C. The ultimate wisdom consists of fearing the Lord.
      1. This means believing in Him, reverencing Him, receiving His truth and serving Him with affectionate obedience.
      2. This type of wisdom not only glorifies God, but it also serves our own highest interests.

II. **What Is Meant By Applying Our Hearts Unto Wisdom**
   A. This involves giving careful thought to our own situation and our own future.
   B. It involves the dilligent use of the various means at our disposal through which we might learn.
      1. Through prayer we are divinely taught and inspired. (Ephesians 1:17)
      2. Through the study of the world round about us we can learn of the greatness of God.
      3. Through the study of the Scriptures, we can learn everything necessary for life and godliness and find the way of salvation made perfectly clear.
      4. Through the study of the dealings of God with us, we can learn the ways of God with man.

III. Why We Should Apply Our Hearts Unto Wisdom
A. Because of the excellency of wisdom. The most important thing is to know the Lord who gives life.
B. Because of the brevity and uncertainty of life. We have such a short life span that we need to learn to make good use of our time and opportunities.
C. Because death ends the last opportunity. Scripture gives us no reason at all to believe that there is any opportunity at all after the grave to settle what we failed to settle in life.
D. Because of the eternal issues involved. If we are wise unto salvation, we shall be happy both here and hereafter.

Conclusion:

The fool fails to learn from the lessons of life. If we would be wise men, we cannot face the death of a friend or loved one without a willingness to learn from this event. The greatest thing we can learn is to have wisdom enough to trust Christ.

—Adapted from F.G. Curtis

Our Great God

PSALM 111

Introduction:

Our hearts melt with sorrow; our eyes run down with tears, and our very souls are troubled within us. Truly we need a touch of the greatness of our great God. This wonderful passage tells us four helpful things about our great God that should comfort us at this time of sorrow.

I. **God Shows Great Wisdom Through His Works. (1-4a, 7 & 8)**

   A. The words of God are readily manifest for all to see, especially those who seek to see them.
   B. These works show much of what God is like.
      1. They stress His greatness.
      2. They powerfully point out His enormous wisdom.
      3. His wisdom encourages us in sorrow.
   C. These works of God are permanent and unchanging.

II. **God Shows Great Compassion In His Dealings. (4b & 5)**

   A. His compassion is so great that He is described as being "full of compassion".
   B. We are told that He has supplied the needs of those who wait on Him.
   C. God is consistently faithful to His promises to be compassionate.

III. **God Shows Great Power In His World. (6)**

   A. He has demonstrated this to His people.
      1. They are the ones to whom it is shown.
      2. They are the ones who best understand it.
   B. The people of God are thus assured that the heritage of all the nations will ultimately be theirs.

IV. **God Shows Great Redemption In His Word. (9 & 10)**

   A. God has provided redemption for His people.
   B. This is found through the "fear of the Lord".
      1. This is the Old Testament expression for faith or belief.

      2.   It is at the point of belief in Christ that wisdom begins.

C.   Those who enter into this relationship are assured of good understanding and eternal favor.

Conclusion:

May the touch of the greatness of our great God serve as a means of lifting the veil of sorrow and drying the tears from our eyes as well as calming our troubled souls.

God Comforts His Pilgrim Children

ISAIAH 43:1-3

Introduction:
No matter how permanent the home of life of a man may seem, we are in reality all pilgrims moving through this life in temporary dwellings. One of these trying experiences is to see another pilgrim called up to the celestial city. It is at such times that we are reminded that God comforts His pilgrim children.

I. **Our Pilgrimage Subjects Us To Trying Experiences.**
   A. There is no possible means of escaping them. They are the inevitable result of the conditions of life in which we find ourselves.
   B. At some point for each one of us, the waters get a bit deeper and the flames a bit higher.
   C. These unavoidable trying experiences subject us to fear and uncertainty that is most disturbing.

II. **God Gives His Pilgrims Many Grounds Of Comfort.**
   A. He says to us, "Fear not, for I am with thee." (Psalm 23:4)
      1. He walks with us even in the darkest valley.
      2. His arm is ever around us and His resources ever at our disposal.
   B. We depend on God's care for He has a fatherly interest in us.
      1. We are His children by creation.
      2. We are His children by His call.
      3. We are His children by the great purchase of redemption.
   C. This ought to be sufficient grounds to give us great confidence.
   D. We can see all this worked out in the experience of ancient Israel, and this should cause us to take even greater courage.

III. **God Comforts His Pilgrims In The Hour Of Bereavement.**
   A. We can apply the text to the deceased or to those who mourn if all know the Lord.

B. We can take to heart the precious promises of the text:
1. Fear not.
2. I have redeemed thee.
3. Thou art mine.
4. I am your Saviour.
C. We can also take comfort from the fact that our loss is the gain of the one we have lost.

Conclusion:

The truth of our text may be of personal comfort because we can see ourselves as pilgrims on a road that is often difficult. May we find the pilgrim's God sufficient for the pilgrim's pathway.

—Adapted from Golladay

The Uncertainty Of Life

MARK 13:33

Introduction:

The veiling of the future is a merciful dispensation of Providence. It is best for man that it should be so. Even in the face of death there is a sense in which it is best that our future is known only to God.

There is, however, a real need for us to look wisely to that which is sure and certain about the future.

I. **The Fact Of Life's Uncertainty.**
   A. The most sure thing in life is one of its most uncertain — death.
      1. Man is born to die, and death is inevitable.
      2. Man's own very inward nature teaches him to sense impending death.
   B. The certainty of death has the uncertainty of its time.
      1. Men are called to account in the midst of the business of life.
      2. Men are called to account in the midst of their sin and rebellion against God.
      3. Even the righteous and holy must recognize the uncertainty of the time when the summons will come.

II. **The Duty Taught By Life's Uncertainty.**
   A. "Take ye heed."
      1. Give thought to the ultimacy of life and death.
      2. Make preparation while there is still time and life.
   B. "Watch and pray."
      1. Live habitually prepared for the end.
      2. Never live in such a way that the end would catch you totally unprepared.

III. **The Answer To Life's Uncertainty.**
   A. Trust in Christ.
      1. He is all in all.
      2. All preparation for eternity lies right here.
   B. Habitually commune with God.

      1.   This is made possible only for the one who is converted.

      2.   This is constant intercourse of the soul with God.

C.   Habitually aim at Christian consistency.

      1.   This is possible only for the one who is truly Christian.

      2.   Our religion begins with God and extends to society.

Conclusion:

Herein is a warning to those who are neither watching nor praying.

Herein is a reproof to the lukewarm professor and the backslider.

Herein is encouragement to the earnest, expectant, watching believer.

—Adapted

The Importance Of Preparation

MARK 13:35-36

Introduction:
The great lesson for us to be learned from this text is that we should always be ready for death. This tabernacle must be dissolved. We should be ready for the event. Since so much has been done for man, preparation is possible. If preparation is not made, sad will be the results. If the soul is prepared, grand will be the results.

I. **Preparation Is Possible.**
  A. Provisions have been made for man's instruction.
    1. The light of nature.
    2. The Word of God.
    3. The minstry of the Holy Spirit.
  B. Provision has been made for man's cleansing through the blood of Jesus Christ.
  C. Provision has been made for man's spiritual development through the laws of growth worked out in the Word of God.

II. **Neglected Preparation Is Sad.**
  A. Death is a sad event for the unprepared man for it is the "funeral of the soul".
  B. The condition of the unprepared man is miserable.
    1. He faces intense suffering.
    2. He faces the agony of remembering:
      a. The great salvation neglected.
      b. The good that he might have done.
      c. The condition that he might have been in.
  C. The unprepared man is unfit for heaven.
    1. He is rejected because of impurity.
    2. He is unfit for the higher service.
    3. He would be out of place in the celestial surroundings.
  D. The unprepared man is in a hopeless state — lost forever.

III. **Preparation Has Glorious Results.**
  A. Death is a happy event to the prepared man.
    1. Beautiful scenes meet his eyes.

2. He faces a happy home with a glorified Christ and saints in glory.
B. The prepared man is in a happy condition:
   1. Fulness of joy.
   2. Pefect peace.
   3. Endless bliss.
C. The prepared man has the best preparation — he is prepared for heaven.
   1. He is ready and fit for higher service.
   2. He is in harmony with the celestial surroundings.
   3. He finds kindred spirits there — heaven is home.

Conclusion:

How carefully we should live, ever seeking the preparation that is necessary. Nothing else can take its place. No grand funeral nor eloquent funeral address by some eloquent divine, nor flattering obituary written by a friend, can take the place of that preparation which should have been made.

—Allshouse

The Gift Of God's Love

JOHN 3:16

Introduction:

There are many subjects on which one may profitably speak at a time like this. There are few subjects so rich in thought, that put such a solid foundation under one's feet, especially at a time like this, as that presented by this little text. Let us ponder:

I. **The Greatness Of God's Love.**
   A. All good gifts are from God. (James 1:17)
   B. This is the greatest gift of all - His only begotten Son.
   C. And He gave Him, not to occupy a throne here, but to suffer and die.

II. **The Universality of God's Love.**
   A. Not only for Israel, His own chosen people.
   B. Not for some elite to whom He was especially attached.
   C. For all mankind, lost, perishing.

III. **The Purpose of God's Love.**
   A. Not to glorify or make a name for the giver.
   B. To save the lost, the perishing.
   C. To secure to those for whom given, eternal life and a home with the Giver in heaven.

IV. **The Condition of Receiving God's Love.**
   A. Not by purchase, were each a billionaire.
   B. Not by mere intellectual apprehension.
   C. By simple acceptance by faith.

V. **The Reassurance Of It.**
   A. If, when men were strangers and aliens, unloving and unlovely, God gave such a gift to men,
   B. Is there anything God will fail to give to those who have accepted this gift?
   C. Can we not trust our dead to such a God?

Conclusion:

May the love of God as expressed in the Word of God cause us to take heart and find encouragement even in the midst of the discouraging.

—Golladay

A Glimpse Of The Heart Of God

JOHN 3:16

Introduction:

By a glimpse of the heart of God, I do not mean a mere fleeting, tantalizing vision of God. This little text, directly or by implication, presents about all that is known of God, so far as His relation to humanity is concerned. It presents truths before the magnitude of which angels bow and worship.

I. **The Heart Of God Is A Heart Of Love.**
   A. There are many who feel that God is distant and unknowable.
   B. This passage tells us that God is not only knowable, but that He also shows Himself to us through love.
   C. The beauty and richness of His love is shown by what He did for us.
      1. His love was sacrificial.
      2. His love was a giving of Himself.
      3. His love involved the giving of the very best possible.

II. **The Heart Of God Is A Heart Of Universal Love.**
   A. Human love is limited by a multitude of different factors which basically involve man's humanity.
   B. God's love is totally universal.
      1. It extends to the whole world.
      2. It encompasses both His friends and His enemies.
      3. It transcends all barriers of any kind.

III. **The Heart Of God Is A Heart Of Purposeful Love.**
   A. Human love is often selfish in purpose. We love for what we might get in return from those we love.
   B. God's love desires every blessing for those whom He loves.
      1. Salvation from perishing.
      2. The gift of eternal life.
      3. The restoration of the likeness of God in man.
      4. Perfection, blessedness and glory.

IV. The Heart Of God Is A Heart Of Giving Love.
A. His love can not be purchased with all the wealth in the world.
B. His love is accepted by faith alone, by accepting the gift which is proffered.

Conclusion:

With a love like this, with a gift like this, with a purpose like this, can we not accept the goodness of the Lord even in the face of sorrow?

—Adapted from Golladay

In My Father's House

Introduction:

Bunyan's *Pilgrim's Progress* is built around the journies and experiences of a pilgrim seeking a heavenly city. Actually we are all pilgrims seeking the heavenly city which our Heavenly Father has promised us.

I. **Looking For A City. (Cf. Hebrews 11:8-10)**
   A. The city we seek is only seen by faith. (vs. 8)
      1. This makes it none-the-less sure.
      2. But it does involve much obedience.
   B. The city we seek causes us to keep our roots shallow. (vs.9)
      1. We are dwelling in a strange place.
      2. We are dwelling in non-permanent lodging.
   C. The city we seek causes us to keep our eyes fixed on heaven. (vs. 10)
      1. The city we seek transposes time.
      2. The city we seek has a builder and maker who is God himself.

II. **The Glory Of That City. (John 14:1-3)**
   A. It is a place prepared by our Lord.
      1. He went away for that specific purpose.
      2. If He helped form such a beautiful world (even beautiful with the sin-scars on it), how much more beautiful the city He prepares for us.
   B. It is a place of great glory.
      1. We really know few of the details about its actual appearance.
      2. We do know that just the presence of the One who has prepared it will make it surpassingly glorious.
   C. It is a place of unique freedom.
      1. We enter it immediately upon death (at least we enter His conscious presence).
      2. There is great freedom promised in His presence. (Revelation 7:16 & 17)

III. **The Way Into That City.** (John 14:3-6)
    A.   Jesus stated it — "I am the Way . . ."
        1.   Would have been blasphemy from anyone else.
        2.   This is from the same One, however, who said, "I am the door."
    B.   The key to the way is found in John 10:9 and Acts 16:31.
        1.   We enter in by belief in Him.
        2.   There is simply no other way of entry. (John 3:3)
    C.   The city and the way are sure — are you?

Conclusion:
Seek the city through Christ, and you will surely find it.

My Home In Heaven

JOHN 14:1-6

Introduction:

At a time when the foundation seems to be shaking, it is good to turn to the Word of God for that sure foundation which never shakes or trembles. I know no better place to turn at a time of sorrow than this splendid passage.

Let us center our thoughts especially on verse 2: "In my Father's house are many mansions . . . I go to prepare a place for you."

I. Consider Our Home On Earth.

A. We are all home builders by nature.

B. People go to almost any length of trouble, effort and sacrifice to secure a home for the present.

C. Our earthly homes are places of refuge and security in the storms of life.

D. No matter how lovely and secure the home, however, it is not at all permanent.

E. This sense of impermanence is one of our profound earthly problems.

II. Consider Our Home In Heaven.

A. There is a *place* prepared for us - something tangible and real.

B. It is located in the place where He has His headquarters.

C. There is going to be plenty of room in the place God is preparing. (Note that Christ speaks of many mansions in the plural).

D. Knowing the One preparing this place for us, causes us to feel that it will be a perfect place.

E. When everything is in a state of perfect readiness, Jesus is going to come for us and take us to that new home.

F. The home to which we look is a permanent one which never passes away.

III. Consider How We Reach That Home.

A. All men reach a future life, but not all men reach heaven.

B. Christ pointed out the way to the disciples.
   1. They professed not to know the way.
   2. Christ said that it was through Him that this home was secured.
C. The one who looks to Jesus as Saviour has the promise of that home.

Conclusion:
How these thoughts should comfort and strengthen our hearts at this time. The one for whom we sorrow and mourn is home, and we are really the ones left adrift and at sea.

—Adapted from Golladay

Life

JOHN 14:19

Introduction

There are few moments in our experience when the real issues of life and death are joined quite as clearly as when we stare into an open grave. We who are living would do well to be sure we understand the meaning of life.

I.   "Yet A Little While And The World Seeth Me No More, But You Shall See Me . . ."
    A. The world wanted to stop seeing Him so they crucified Him.
    B. The world did not see Him again — their efforts were successful — but the disciples did see Him again.

II. ". . .Because I Live . . ."
    A. Christ speaks prophetically of the resurrection as if it had already taken place.
        1. Note His appearances. (I Corinthians 15:5-8)
        2. Note the impact of this fact upon history.
    B. Christ is going to experience a life that is eternal. (Hebrews 7:25)
    C. Stress must be laid on the nature of this resurrection which led to an eternal life for Him.
        1. It was a real resurrection of one who was actually dead.
        2. It was fully supernatural in its method and intent.

III. ". . . Ye Shall Live Also."
    A. The resurrection is of tremendous importance to us.
        1. His deity was thus proven.
        2. Victory over sin was assured for all time. (I Corinthians 15:55-57)
        3. Our resurrection was secured and assured.
    B. The door to eternal life was thrown open to all.
        1. The life which He secured is for time and eternity.
        2. Since He lives in this way, so we too may live.
        3. The only necessity for participation is belief.
    C. All men will again see Christ.

1. Those who didn't want to see Him will see Him in judgment.
2. Those who reject Him will see Him reject them.
3. Those who have received Him will see Him as Saviour and Lord.

Conclusion:

When we come to the time when the issues of life and death are joined, it is comforting to know that because of what He did for us, we may have the absolute assurance of eternal life.

The Peace That The Saviour Can Give

JOHN 14:27

Introduction:
Some of life's least tranquil moments are enacted in funeral homes and at cemeteries. If peace is ever going to desert one, it is likely to happen in the moment of grief. Because of that, it would be well to review this great theme of the peace of God.

I. **The Gift — Peace.**
A. Its nature.
    1. It is not the absence of strife.
        a. Too often confused in this way.
        b. It isn't even harmonious inter-personal relationships.
    2. It is an inner state of calm and order.
        a. It is a quality which appears in the midst of strife.
        b. It does affect relationships with others.
B. Its quality.
    1. It is intimately connected with Christ.
    2. It touches deeply into the Spiritual realm.

II. **The Giver — Christ.**
A. Note the contrast here.
    1. Christ's peace:
        a. Real.
        b. Delivered on promise.
        c. Continuing.
    2. The world's peace:
        a. Unreal
        b. Undependable.
        c. Temporary.
B. Note the character of Christ's peace.
    1. It is the same peace He knew.
    2. Notice these elements:
        a. Calm in turmoil.
        b. Steadiness of purpose.
        c. Rightness with the Father.

III. **The Giving — Left, Given.**
A. It is a gift from Christ.

  1. Peace is received and not worked up.
  2. The peace of Christ thus contrasts with many other philosophies.
  3. We merely need to open our hearts to it.
 B. There is a contrast in the giving.
  1. Christ gives:
   a. Freely.
   b. Fully.
   c. Finally.
  2. The world gives:
   a. Grudgingly (one has to work for it).
   b. Half-heartedly.
   c. Occasionally.

IV. The Goal.

 A. "Let not your heart be troubled."
  1. Do not keep on being stirred up by things.
  2. Know this peace even in the midst of sorrow.
 B. "Neither let it be afraid."
  1. Do not allow fear to find its way into your heart.
  2. Do not allow apprehension to take control.
 C. Know the splendor of His peace.

Conclusion:

There is no necessity for the sorrow of this moment to rob you of the tranquility of your soul. Remember that God gave peace through Christ and that it is yours in spite of circumstances.

And This Is Life Eternal

JOHN 17:1-3

Introduction:
As we stand before the casket and opened grave, we want something of a glimpse into eternity. The opening verses of Christ's prayer in John 17 provide us with the look we desire.

I. **His Heartfelt Petition.** (1)
   A. He prays on the basis of the Father-Son relationship — "Father".
   B. He prays with a recognition of God's appointments — "the hour is now come".
   C. He prays with a specific request — "glorify thy Son". In this He is praying for strength to endure the cross through which He will pass to glorification.
   D. He prays with a specific reason — "in order that Thy Son might glorify thee". Once the cross would be accomplished, greater glory would come to God through Christ.

II. **His Imparted Information.** (2)
   A. The Son will glorify the Father through giving men eternal life.
   B. God has already given Him full authority over all men.
   C. This gift of authority is so that He might give the gift of eternal life to those for whom it is intended.

III. **His Sublime Explanation.** (3)
   A. Eternal life is life unending by its very definition.
   B. Eternal life is life lived in the presence of God. (unending life would not be desirable under other conditions).
   C. Eternal life is life connected with the "true" God.
   D. Eternal life is splendid life.
   E. Eternal life is secured only through Christ. We must know Him to know eternal life.
   F. Eternal life is life known absolutely.

Conclusion:

Here is a look into eternity. Eternity offers eternal life, life full, free, lived in the presence of God. This eternal life is through knowing the Father and the Son. Such life extends beyond the grave.

The Christian's Assured Victory

ROMANS 8:37-39

Introduction:

Death, from the merely natural man's point of view, from all that we can see with the eye of flesh, is failure, going down in defeat. Death topples the crown from the brow of the king; it wrests the scepter from the hand of the potentate in state and church. This, according to mere human reckoning, is failure.

When we take God into account, however, and take His reasoning into account, death is not failure, but victory, earth's last great victory.

I. **The Christian's Conflict.**
   A. Conflict is one of the realities of life, and it affects every area of our experience.
      1. True in national life.
      2. True in the life of the individual.
      3. True in the life of the church.
   B. The one whom we honor had conflicts.
      1. This is true no matter whom we are honoring, and no matter what the situation might be.
      2. If we were to know in truth, the conflict has probably been much greater than we dream.
   C. And now the conflict is over for this one. Now the body lies before us in death. Can we still speak of victory? Do not death and victory nullify one another? NO!!!

II. **The Christian's Victory.**
   A. It is not won by virtue of one's own wisdom, strength or merit.
   B. It is won by virtue of the fact that God is with us and gives us the victory.
   C. Death is not defeat, but victory because only in death does the Christian life really come into its own. It is then that it lays aside its weaknesses and imperfections and becomes glorious and reaches its destiny.
   D. The ground of our assurance for final victory is not guesswork. It is . . .

37

III. The Love Of The Christian's God.

A. "Who or what shall separate us from the love of Christ?"
   1. Nothing in this world can do it.
   2. No power in the spirit world can do it.
   3. Because God loves us, all the resources of His love are enlisted in our favor.
   4. Genuine love such as His is the best guarantee of true faithfulness.

B. This love of God toward us has been amply proved by all He has done, beginning on the cross and extending right up to this point in our lives.

C. God loves us enough to make all things work together for good. Thus this loved one's death is not a defeat but a victory.

D. Our attitude, therefore, ought to be that of those who sorrow *with* hope. We have a sorrow, but it is tempered by the fact that this one has entered into assured victory.

Conclusion:

When we come to a service like this, do we ever have any serious thoughts about that day so sure to come when we shall be at the end of our own earthly life? Are we approaching it with the sense that it is going to be our great day of victory and with the assurance that no powers or experiences of earth, no powers of the spirit world, can separate us from the love of God in Christ?

—Adapted

Eternal Assurance

I CORINTHIANS 15

Introduction:

The sorrowing heart needs assurance concerning eternity. Such assurance is possible when the deceased was a child of God. The assurance comes from the certainly attested fact of the resurrection.

I. The Importance Of The Resurrection. (1-4)
   A. The theme has wide Biblical prominence.
      1. There is much mention of it in the New Testament.
      2. This chapter is the classic Biblical location on the subject.
   B. There is conflict involved in it.
      1. Satan and God are locked in unseen conflict.
      2. Christ died, but to stay dead would be to lose the conflict.
   C. There are historical facts in it.
      1. The resurrection is proved by witnesses as adequate as could ever be expected to testify in a court case.
      2. The resurrection has to stand as one of the best attested facts of human history.

II. The Assurance Of The Resurrection. (20-23)
   A. This involves the principle of "first-fruits".
      1. This is an Old Testament concept.
      2. What it means is that the first grain, etc., is given as a promise that all the rest that is due will be given.
      3. Christ's resurrection thus promises that all who are promised will be brought forth.
   B. The purchase of life is detailed.
      1. All men deserve to die for sin.
      2. As sin comes by one, so life comes by One.

III. The Method Of The Resurrection. (35-38, 42-44)
   A. Illustrated from nature.
      1. Seed must die to grow.

  2. The final product is quite different from what has been planted.
 B. Involves a different body.
  1. The resurrection body is spiritual rather than physical.
  2. The words and phrases are very descriptive.
 C. When all is said, however, we don't actually know the "how" of the resurrection.

IV. The Meaning Of The Resurrection. (54-57)
 A. The strength of death is broken.
  1. Death has lost its sting and finality.
  2. The grave has no victory - becomes merely one way for a believer to enter into life.
 B. The only way to this victory is through the Lord Jesus Christ. (57)
  1. He won the victory; we must share it through Him.
  2. The only way to do this is through receiving Him. (John 3:16)

Conclusion:

When the person we mourn has "died in the Lord", we have great eternal assurance. Each one present can also have that assurance personally.

The Giver Of Grace And Peace

CORINTHIANS 1:3

Introduction:
Sorrow extracts its price. It is well if it is not allowed to continue too long. It is not, however, something which we are able just to "turn off". Help is needed from some source. Paul proposes that given by the Giver of grace and peace.

I. **The Gift.**
   A. Two words of rich meaning.
      1. Grace: All the blessings God bestows on men who don't deserve them.
      2. Peace: Rest and tranquility in the spiritual realm.
   B. Paul wishes to see them intensified.
      1. Corinthians already had grace and peace.
      2. He implies that he wants them to have more.
   C. Two commonplace words are thus rendered uncommon.
      1. Just the usual words for Hebrew and Greek greetings.
      2. Notice how the commonplace becomes uncommon when used by the Lord.

II. **The Giver.**
   A. These come from the Father and the Son.
      1. Stresses their essential equality.
      2. Emphasizes the deity of Christ.
   B. Mention of both indicates both are involved in the bestowal of grace and peace.
      1. They were conceived in the mind of God.
      2. They were made available through the work of Christ.
   C. The mention of the Father and Son as sources of grace and peace exhausts the list of available sources of supply.
      1. Neither grace nor peace is available from any other source.
      2. Every effort of man to find either outside Christ is doomed to absolute failure.

III. The Giving.
A. These are gifts:
   1. There is no way in which they can be earned.
   2. If we could learn this, we could benefit from them so much more.
B. They are given in order:
   1. Grace comes first — first the grace of God must be known.
   2. Then comes peace — peace follows where grace abounds.

Conclusion:
The help needed in sorrow can be found in the giver of grace and peace.

Sanctified Affliction

II CORINTHIANS 4:17

Introduction:
The Apostle's state of mind was truly a happy one. He was able to endure manifold afflictions and privations with patience and contentment, and to think of them as tending to promote high and holy purposes. He enumerates some of those afflictions, and then he sees beyond these the rest and glory upon which he will enter when they are passed away.

I. **The Christian's Estimate of Afflictions**
   A. The word comes from one that means: something that beats down, presses sore and is in itself grievous and tormenting.
   B. The forms of human trial are very diversified.:
      1. Bodily sufferings.
      2. Seasons of providential darkness.
      3. Times of trial and tempest.
      4. Trials due to spiritual adversaries and weapons.
   C. This affliction in its diversified form is the inevitable lot of man.
   D. Paul views it through another light:
      1. It is of short duration.
      2. It is light in importance.
      3. The eyes of faith see above the gloom and cloud.

II. **The Beneficial Tendency of Affliction**
   A. Affliction "works" to prepare us for something else — an eternal weight of glory.
   B. It is designed to:

      1. Correct and reclaim our wandering.

      2. Promote spiritual advantage.

      3. Subdue the mind by breaking pride.

      4. Refine, elevate and purify the Christian character.
   C. In reality faith gains through trial. The Christian is made a happier, holier and better man for it.

III. The Glory For Which Affliction Prepares

A. It is described as, "A far more exceeding and eternal weight of glory."

B. The beauty and sublimity of heavenly glory surpasses our highest conception of it:

    1. There are different states or degrees of glory in heaven.

    2. The glory to which we are heading is eternal in its duration.

        a. This is secured by the eternity of the One who secured it.

        b. This is a result of the inviolable fidelity and love of the One who has promised it.

    3. Its degree will be limited only in the capacity of the recipient to receive it.

C. The glory to which we are headed is referred to as a "weight." This speaks of the fact that precious things often have weight.

Conclusion:

We should strive to improve the times of sorrow by learning humility and by a renewed consecration of ourselves to God.

—Adapted

The Christian's Twofold Gain

PHILIPPIANS 1:21

Introduction:

The Apostle Paul was able to view death with great ambivalence. He could see the gain of death and see the gain of life and keep both in full perspective. At this time of death, let us look at the twofold gain of the Christian life and death.

I. **The Christian's Gain In Life.**
   A. The Biblical view of life is not gloomy and unreal.
      1. Jesus was not a gloomy ascetic and did not teach men to be such.
      2. God has given us life, and we should live it to the full.
      3. The Christian has been put in touch with resources of understanding and appreciation which should make him enjoy life even more than anyone else.

   B. The greatest gain of life, however, belongs to the one who has learned to find life's greatest lesson — his need of a Saviour.
   C. The real gain of life is thus the portion of the one who has found newness of life in the only One who can grant newness. If life offered nothing else than finding Christ, it would be worthwhile for this man to have lived.
   D. Once this gain in life has been found, there is nothing in this world that can take it away. He was come to give us life and to make that life more abundant. Part of its abundance is the fact that it can't be taken away.

II. **The Christian's Gain In Death.**
   A. Here is the point where human understanding balks. The natural man cannot see where death is any gain in most cases.
   B. There is real gain to man through death:
      1. He lays aside all his temptations and infirmities.
      2. The cares of life no longer vex him.

3. He becomes perfect, the mortal made immortal and the imperfections wiped away.
4. He enters the presence of His Lord to dwell forever.

C. Although the valley of the shadow is sometimes marked by a bit of uncertainty, the death of the saint is gain of the highest order.

D. Even the thought of leaving behind friends and loved ones can't blot out the glory of the gain from death.

Conclusion:

Let us be wise enough to make gain of both worlds. But let us so live in faith that the gain here, however great it may be, will be as nothing to the gain over there. The gain here is but for a little while. The gain over there is forever.

—Adapted from Golladay

The Hope Of Ultimate Reunion

I THESSALONIANS 4:13-18

Introduction:
The Thessalonians had recently received the Gospel. Since then some of their friends had died. As they had expected to remain in the body until the return of the Lord, and because some of their number had died, they were greatly disturbed. The Apostle includes this passage as a means of comforting their agitation regarding the dead in Christ.

I. **There Will Be A Reunion.**
   A. The dead have not perished.
   B. The separation will not be eternal.
   C. The living shall not precede the dead into eternal fellowship with the Lord Jesus for both shall be caught up into the clouds and both shall live forever with the Lord.

II. **The Hoped For Reunion Shall Be Realized.**
   A. It is founded on the living Christ (verse 14). Actually the resurrection of the Lord Himself becomes the ground of hope for the believer.
   B. It is founded on the Lord's promised and expected return. (Cf. 1:10; Acts 1:10 & 11)

III. **The Hoped For Reunion Shall Be Realized**
   A. This will come when the Lord descends from heaven with glory and great power. (verse 16; also cf., Matthew 24:30 & 31)
   B. Several things will happen then:
      1. The spirits of the righteous will be brought with Him.
      2. The dead will be raised. In order for this to happen, the dead will be raised with incorruptible, glorious, powerful and spiritual bodies.
      3. The living will be transformed. (cf., I Corinthians 15:51-57)

IV. **The Consolation Of The Hoped For Reunion.**
  A. From this we can draw great consolation. The believer in Jesus may mourn, but it should not be as those without hope.
  B. Do you believe all the Bible teaches about the resurrection of Christ and the saints? If so, let it comfort you.
  C. Do you expect the Lord's return? If so, live in the hope of it.

Conclusion:

We have the hope of glorious reunion with our friends in the future if they were in the Lord and we are in the Lord.

—Adapted from J.P. Caldwell

Sorrow, Sleep And A Shout

I THESSALONIANS 4:13-18

Introduction:
The question of the second coming has always been one of great interest to the Saints. This was especially true in the city of Thessalonica where great concern had arisen about the fate of those who die prior to the return of Christ. Paul sets their minds at ease and, at the same time, comforts us.

I. The Background Of The Teaching.
   A. This comes at a most hopeless day in history.
   B. Comes to a church confused on doctrine of death and last things.
      1. Evidently they expected immediate return of Christ.
      2. Some had died without seeing it.
      3. They questioned the effect death would have on the second coming.
   C. The questions of the Thessalonians were leading them to an excessive sorrow (even as they may lead us to the same).

II. The Correction In The Teaching. (13)
   A. "I would not have you to be ignorant . . ."
      1. Statement designed to draw attention.
      2. An indication that they were ignorant in this area.
   B. Puts limit on sorrow.
      1. Does not forbid sorrow.
      2. Points out that it is to be of a different nature from that of the heathen.
   C. Introduces the idea of "hope".
      1. This is a confident expectation of a sure thing.
      2. It is hope that makes the difference in the way we sorrow.

III. The Certainty Of The Teaching. (14)
   A. The hope is based on the resurrection of Christ.
      1. They had believed in this to become Christians.
      2. There is no hope without it. (I Corinthians 15:13-19)

B. The resurrection of Jesus guarantees that of others.
   1. God has brought Him forth.
   2. God is bound to bring others with Him.
   3. This is based on I Corinthians 15:20-23.
C. So we can get our start at the certainty of the resurrection.

IV. The Details Of The Teaching. (15-17)
A. It gets to the heart of the question — how about the dead?
B. Presents basic facts:
   1. There will be saints alive at His coming. (vs. 15)
   2. Those who are alive will have no advantage over the dead. (vs. 15)
   3. Those who are alive will have no preference over the dead.
C. The order of events.
   1. The Lord shall descend from heaven. (16)
   2. The dead in Christ shall rise first. (16b)
   3. The living will be caught up together with them. (17)
   4. Together they shall meet the Lord in the air. (17)
   5. All shall be with Him forever. (17)

V. The Purpose Of The Teaching. (18)
A. To meet need.
   1. Answers specific questions.
   2. Provides additional details.
B. To point out a difference.
   1. This is for the ones in Christ.
   2. It clearly reveals the need of accepting the Saviour.
C. To provide comfort for the sorrowing.
   1. Not just to keep them from fainting.
   2. Actually designed to provide positive encouragement.
      a. Concerning our dead loved ones.
      b. Concerning our own future.

Conclusion:
Here is great comfort for those at the side of an open grave. The Lord is coming again, and all of us who know Him are going to be reunited with Him by that coming.

Heaven, A Better Country

HEBREWS 11:16

Introduction:

From time immemorial men have sought for a "better country" than this fleeting, passing life. The Bible clearly points out heaven as being that very thing — a better country.

I. **Heaven Is A Better Place.**
   A. It is a more exalted country.
      1. It is the place of the throne of God.
      2. It is the court of the multitudes of angels.
   B. It is a more holy country.
      1. It is not marred by sin.
      2. It is a place of completed moral freedom for its residents.
   C. It is a more heathful country.
      1. Sin, the great causer of disease, is not there.
      2. Its inhabitants are free from bodily, spiritual and mental afflictions.
   D. It is a more happy country.
      1. Sources of disquietude, fear and grief and unknown.
      2. It is a place where there is nothing to make one unhappy.
   E. It is a more abiding country.
      1. There we shall be residents rather than pilgrims.
      2. Heaven is a kingdom which does not fade at all like earthly kingdoms.
   F. It is a better country.
      1. It is the region of perfect and consummate glory.
      2. The place of perfect enjoyment, security, employments, etc.

II. **Heaven Is A Desirable Place.**
   A. Believers have secured title to it.
      1. By faith in Christ they have become heirs of heaven.
      2. They are those whose names are written there.
   B. Believers are striving for a "meetness" to enjoy it.

  1. It is a heavenly country, and they are seeking for a growing heavenliness.

  2. They are learning now the fellowship which they will enjoy then.

C. Believers labor and pray for it.

  1. They seek grace to keep them on the pathway toward it.

  2. They pray for the day when it will be realized.

D. Believers live in the hope of its eternal enjoyment.

  1. They seek the company of heaven-bound fellow travelers.

  2. They speak of the glories of that kingdom with a glow.

Conclusion:

  We seek for a country that is better. We find it in heaven.

            —Adapted

Man's Earthly Mode Of Being

II PETER 1:13-15

Introduction:

We have here a view of our earthly mode of being. The body is not us, but it is ours - our residence, a residence not built of marble and founded on a rock, but a temporary booth pitched here during our short pilgrimage.

I. **There Is A Duty Connected With This Mode Of Being.**
    A. The Apostle saw his work as involving the spiritual excitation of the Christian soul.
    B. He sought to put the Christian in mind of five things:
        1. That spiritual excellency is the great end of Christianity (verses 3 & 4).
        2. That spiritual excellence is progressive in its nature (verses 5 & 7).
        3. That spiritual excellence requires very dilligent exercise (verses 5 & 10).
        4. That spiritual excellence is the only guarantee of salvation (verse 9).
        5. That spiritual excellence will utimately meet with glorious reward (verse 11).
    C. There are three important things implied in the Apostle's aim:
        1. The paramount necessity for the Christian to feel the obligation of these things.
        2. The sad tendency of the Christian to forget these things.
        3. The obligation which the Christian has to seek to excite others by means of these things.

II. **There Is A Destined Change That Awaits This Mode Of Being.**
    A. The nature of the change: it is a putting off of the tabernacle.
    B. The nearness of the change - note the word "shortly".
    C. The assurance of the change - "knowing" means it is not a subject of any doubt.

III. **There Is A Glorious Cause That Must Outlive This Mode Of Being.**
   A.   The Apostle says, "Moreover I will endeavor that ye may be able after my decease to have these things always in remembrance." In this he stresses the importance of the cause to which he has committed outliving the short span of his life.
   B.   His concern for posterity involved three things:
   1.   That Christianity is necessary for posterity. All generations require it, and it must be handed down.
   2.   That Christianity is the greatest good which can be handed down to posterity.
   3.   That a man may greatly help posterity by that which he hands down both by life and record.

Conclusion:

Each man must make a proper estimate of life if he is going to accomplish what God has intended for him. It is at a time of death that we are so plainly reminded to make that proper estimate before the course of life has been run fully.

—David Thomas

Faithful Unto Death

Introduction:

Christ was and is faithful to the interests of His people. Even in the dark moment of sorrow, we can ever rest assured of His continuing interest in us and our needs.

I. **The Text Implies Obligations To Christ's Service.**
   A. We are obligated to Christ's service because of His boundless excellency.
   B. We are obligated to Christ's service by His right of property in us:
      1. He created us.
      2. He redeemed us.
      3. He created us anew.
   C. We are obligated to His service by our covenants and promises made to the Lord at various times during our lives.

II. **The Text Implies Temptations To Unfaithfulness.**
   A. His service often proves difficult to mere flesh and blood.
   B. We are constantly offered a large bribe to desert and betray - that bribe being the world.
   C. Many times we are allured away by such things as positive persecution.

III. **The Text Furnishes The Measure Of Faithfulness — Death.**
   A. This test has so often been applied to men.
   B. Christian faithfulness has ever withstood it.
   C. In fact, it often seems that we yield to much lesser tests and stand the hard test of potential death.

IV. **The Text Implies That The Trial Of Faithfulness Shall Cease With Time.**
   A. There is no corruption in heaven.
   B. There is no misrepresentation in heaven.
   C. There is no tempter in heaven.

V. **The Text Reveals The Reward Of Faithfulness.**
   A. A crown - honor, dominion.

B. A crown of life - a living, lasting crown.

C. This is a reward in proportion to the investment of life involved.

VI. The Text Connects Time With Eternity.

A. We are forced to think of going and leaving all behind.

B. We are reminded that the past is already there.

C. We are forced to admit that we weave our own destiny.

VII. The Text Shows The Author Of This Connection.

A. The omniscient Christ.

B. The unchangeable Christ.

C. The omnipotent Christ.

D. The equitable Christ.

Conclusion:

At the time of the death of a faithful servant of Christ, we are both comforted and confronted by the Biblical promise of the reward of faithfulness to the Lord Jesus Christ.

—James Stewart

No Tears In Heaven

REVELATION 21:4

Introduction:
Those passing through the time of sorrow seldom need reminding of the frequency and tragedy of human tears. The Bible, however, points to a time when there shall be no more tears by direct act of God.

I. **There Are Tears On Earth.**
   A. This is a well attested fact.
      1. Part of the experience of living.
      2. Amply illustrated right at this particular time.
   B. Those tears have many causes.
      1. Sometimes caused by temporal depression.
      2. Sometimes caused by defective friendships.
      3. Sometimes caused by bitter affliction.
      4. Often caused by bereavements.
      5. Not infrequently caused by our own sense of moral imperfection.

II. **There Shall Be No Tears In Heaven.**
   A. What place is spoken of? Heaven.
      2. This is God's own dwelling place.
      2. This is the Canaan to which we point.
   B. Who shall wipe tears away? God.
      1. The removal of tears is by divine decree.
      2. Notice:
         a. His infinite love insures it.
         b. His infinite power will accomplish it.
         c. The immutability of His promise assures it.
   C. When will He do it? He shall.
      1. It is a promise that is future.
      2. He often wipes away tears now, but He will always do it then.
   D. How will He do it?
      1. He will do it affectionately.
      2. He will do it effectively — all tears.
      3. He will do it certainly. The language is positive.

Conclusion:

The removal of tears implies the enjoyment of positive good. This is exactly what God promises His people. Are you one of them?

—Adapted

No Night

Introduction:

Jesus Christ is appropriately called the Sun of Righteousness. Fixed in the horizon of the universe, He is the light of heaven. Hence it is said of the celestial world in the text, "There shall be no night there".

I. There Shall Be No Natural Or Physical Night There

A. For our present constitution, the alternation of night and day is both desirable and necessary.

B. In heaven the nature of man shall be perfected, and he shall be involved in serving the Lord both night and day.

C. The absence of night there provides for a greater amount of service and an uninterrupted enjoyment of pleasure.

II. There Shall Be No Intellectual Night There

A. In this life we have problems with our minds:
   1. They are so long immature.
   2. They are so clouded by disease.
   3. They are trammeled by prejudice.
   4. They are limited by their range of observation.

B. In heaven our minds will be set free:
   1. They will be fully mature.
   2. They will suffer from no disease-produced clouds.
   3. They will know no prejudices.
   4. They will have unlimited observation.

III. There Shall Be No Moral And Spiritual Night There

A. By moral and spiritual night is meant the concealment of distinctions between right and wrong and the concealment of God Himself.

B. In the moral world:
   1. God in His moral attributes is the object.
   2. Christ is the light in which He Himself is seen.
   3. Holiness and union are the powers of vision.

C. In this present world, we are in moral night. In heaven, there will be eternal moral day.

IV. There Shall Be No Providential Night There

A By providential night, we mean the difficulty of seeing God and His government in the passing of events.

B. The providence of God is mixed now as far as we are concerned.

C. In heaven the providence of God will be clearly unfolded and open for the eyes of all to see.

V. There Shall Be No Night Of Affliction And Death There

A. Death is punishment. This cannot be for those who have passed into heaven through the blood of the Lamb.

B. Affliction is discipline. Such discipline will be no longer needed when we reach our state of perfection in Him.

Conclusion:

The glorious place to which the Christian is bound is a place where night shall not exist in any of its forms. What a glorious place! Are you sure you are bound for such a place?

—James Stewart

Death In The Bible

Introduction:

The Bible has a great deal to say about death, and yet its treatment of death is somewhat striking. There are many lessons to be learned from the Biblical treatment of the subject.

I. **Death Is Not Prominent In The Bible.**
   A. There are so many men whose deaths are not even mentioned. (e.g., Peter, Paul and John)
   B. The great themes of the Bible run counter to death.
      1. Life — its duties, responsibilities and destiny.
      2. Eternity — its rewards and penalties.
      3. The atonement — its means of escaping the penalty of sin.

II. **Death Is Seen As A Putting Off Of A Tabernacle.**
   A. It is sometimes viewed as a disrobing.
      1. It is putting off the mortal.
      2. It is laying aside the infirmities, suffering and pain.
   B. It is elsewhere viewed as a putting on of something.
      1. Mortality is taken off and immortality is put on.
      2. There is a picture of getting out of the old and into the new.

III. **Death Is Viewed From A Heavenly Viewpoint.**
   A. It is described as an abundant entrance. (II Peter 1:11)
   B. It is viewed as a glorious reception. (John 14:3)

IV. **Death Is Shown To Have No Effect Upon The Soul.**
   A. The disrobing, departure and laying aside aspects only affect the body and not the soul.
   B. The soul is uniformly looked upon as living on regardless of the changes which come to pass in the body.

V. **Death Is Viewed As A Great Exaltation.**
   A. One goes from the old, worn and tattered to the new and glorious.
   B. This is merely the passing from the temporal and limited to the eternal and unlimited.

Conclusion:

Much of the sting is taken from death when we have the Biblical perspective concerning it.

—S.W. Fellows

Reflections On The Death Of A Little Child

Introduction:

One of the most painful experiences that life affords is that of the homegoing of a little one. How fortunate we are at a time like this to know certain facts that the Word of God teaches us.

I. **Christ Called Little Ones To Him (Mark 10:14)**
   A. While on earth, He desired the company of little ones.
   B. The little one whom we mourn has been called to Him. Although we surely don't know why, we are assured that such is the case.
   C. We are sure that little ones go to be with Him at death for the following reasons:
      1. If He desired their company on earth, it is likely that He would also in heaven.
      2. The story of David's lamentation for the son of Bathsheba also instructs us.
      3. We believe that little ones who are not yet old enough to understand their need of salvation go to be with the Lord when they die.

II. **Christ Used Little Ones To Teach (Matthew 18:1-6)**
   A. He used the little child to teach:
      1. Humility.
      2. Simplicity.
      3. The true meaning of faith.
   B. We can use the death of a little child as a teaching experience and learn the following from it:
      1. How very fragile life — it takes so little to snuff it out.
      2. How very uncertain life — we are always but a step from death.
      3. How very brief life is — this child's life is so short in comparison to ours; our life is so short in comparison to eternity.
   C. We must learn from the death of a little child to number our days wisely and apply our hearts to wisdom while we have life.

III. **Christ Spoke Of Little Ones As Pointing The Way To Heaven (Matthew 18:3)**
   A. We must be aware of the fact that not all adults go to heaven.
   B. Heaven is secured by a certain "child-likeness".
      1. We need the child's sense of dependency to show us our need of help from without ourselves.
      2. We need the child's simplicity to enable us to accept something which seems so simple.
      3. We need the child's simple faith to accept the salvation which God so freely offers.
   C. "Becoming as a little child" actually is simply a matter of the exercise of child-like qualities in response to God.

Conclusion:

The death of a little child is not in vain if from it we learn to apply our hearts to wisdom and exercise child-like qualities in regard to our relationship with God.